ORPINGTON TO TONBRIDGE

including the BRANCH LINE TO WESTERHAM

Vic Mitchell and Keith Smith

MP Middleton Press

First published June 1992

ISBN 1 873793 03 0

Typesetting - Barbara Mitchell
Design   - Deborah Goodridge

Published by Middleton Press
            Easebourne Lane
            Midhurst
            West Sussex
            GU29 9AZ
            Tel: (0730) 813169

Printed & bound by Biddles Ltd,
            Guildford and Kings Lynn

CONTENTS

53	Brasted
13	Chelsfield
49	Chevening Halt
34	Dunton Green
94	Hildenborough
21	Knockholt
71	Sevenoaks
103	Tonbridge
116	Tonbridge Shed
1	Orpington
57	Westerham

ACKNOWLEDGEMENTS

Our deep gratitude goes to many of the photographers mentioned in the credits who have provided much detailed information. The same sentiment is expressed to R.M.Casserley, Dr.E.Course, G.Croughton, A.Dasi-Sutton, K.Dungate, C.Hall, P.Hay, Dr.S.Huber, N.Langridge, Rev.H.Mace, D.Pede, R.Randell, D.Salter, E.Staff, N.Stanyon, Miss M.Wheeller and our ever supportive wives.

The 1955 route diagram, showing the electrified routes with bold lines.

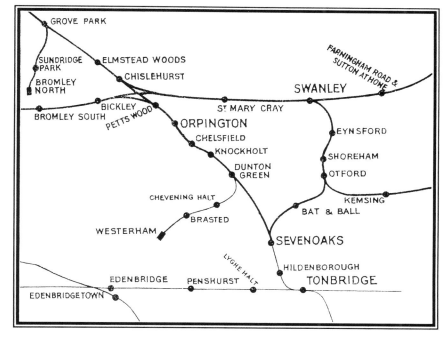

GEOGRAPHICAL SETTING

Having climbed all the way from London, the route continues to rise on the Chalk of the dip slope of the North Downs to Knockholt. The line descends through Polhill Tunnel onto the scarp slope and crosses a mile of Gault Clay in the vicinity of Dunton Green. Here it then traverses the Darent Valley, along which ran the branch line to Westerham.

At Sevenoaks, the route climbs onto the sands of the Hythe Beds and tunnels through them into Wealden Clay. The build up of water in the sand above the clay resulted in expensive tunnelling, continuing instability, and water penetration problems.

The Wealden Clay is traversed for about three miles as the line descends into the valley of the Upper Medway and joins the Redhill-Ashford route after crossing this river. Tonbridge station is built on Brickearth bordering the south side of the valley.

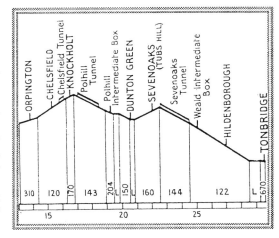

All maps are to the scale of 25" to 1 mile, unless otherwise inscribed.

HISTORICAL BACKGROUND

The line between Chislehurst and Sevenoaks was authorised on 30th August 1862, opened on 2nd March 1868 and extended to Tonbridge on 1st May of that year. It was built by the South Eastern Railway to reduce the distance between London and Dover, as until then its trains had to travel via the 1842 Redhill route. The "New Main Line" gave a reduction of 24 miles. Local traffic gradually grew and made this expensive line more remunerative.

A link to the London Chatham & Dover Railway's 1862 route to Sevenoaks (Bat & Ball) was established on 1st August 1869, but there were subsequently two periods of closure, described later.

After several fruitless attempts, a branch from Dunton Green to Westerham was authorised on 24th July 1876 and opened on 7th July 1881. The SER acquired it three weeks later. After a peaceful existence, it closed on 30th October 1961.

The SER and the LCDR were operated as one from 1st January 1899, becoming known as the South Eastern & Chatham Railway. This became part of the Southern Railway in 1923, which in turn formed the Southern Region of British Railways upon nationalisation in 1948.

Electrification between London and Orpington took place in 1925-26, the route onwards to Sevenoaks carrying local electric services from 6th January 1935. Extension of third-rail operation to Tonbridge took place on 12th June 1961, when electric services to Dover commenced.

Westerham Valley Association

This was formed in 1962 as a result of the merger of the Westerham Branch Railway Passengers' Association with the Westerham Valley Railway Society. It was proposed to operate a diesel railcar service for commuters, with steam trains at weekends. Three ex-GWR railcars were inspected.

A lease was taken on the station at Westerham and later on that at Brasted. A telephone link was established between them and much work on the buildings and track was undertaken. Rolling stock purchased, mostly by individual members, included three ex-Metropolitan Railway coaches, an ex-SECR brake third and H class 0-4-4T no.31263.

Sadly road building schemes were given priority, the track being lifted and the buildings demolished in 1966. Thus the scheme became one of the great lost causes of railway preservation and the stock went to other private lines.

PASSENGER SERVICES

These notes are restricted to down trains calling at Sevenoaks. Initially there were four slow trains and one express on weekdays.

By June 1869, there were nine trains calling at Sevenoaks on weekdays, but only four of these stopped at Orpington. On Sundays there were two expresses and one train calling at all stations on the route.

By 1890, there were 19 weekday trains from London to Sevenoaks, two of which terminated there. On Sundays there were four slow trains only.

The July 1906 timetable showed 29 services calling at Sevenoaks, their stopping pattern being very variable. Sundays saw 15 trains, the 9.5am offering cheap fares to Margate and Ramsgate.

Apart from some reductions in the latter part of World War I, there was a modest increase to 35 weekday trains up to the advent of local electric services in 1935. Electrification resulted in the introduction of a 30-minute interval local service, in addition to 29 steam trains to Tonbridge or beyond (12 on Sundays).

Dieselisation of Hastings services in 1958 and electrification of the Sevenoaks-Dover route in 1961 resulted in the basic timetable offering an hourly train to Hastings from Sevenoaks, but only a few stopped for Dover passengers. A revision in 1976 resulted in hourly trains to Ashford, to Hastings and to Margate, the local service north of Sevenoaks being reduced to one hourly.

Westerham Branch

The first timetable showed eleven trains on weekdays and eight on Sundays. By 1890 this had been adjusted to twelve and five. An 8.40am through train to Cannon Street was introduced prior to 1900.

Steam railcars came to the branch in April 1906 and operated 14 weekday trips (9 on Sundays), but the 7.25am and 8.38am departures trom Westerham were loco hauled and ran through to Cannon Street. For several years the 5.5pm from Cannon Street had through coaches detached at Dunton Green for Westerham..

Apart from reduction of service during WWI and the Depression of the early 1930s, the timetables to 1934 showed about 17 weekday and 11 Sunday journeys. Electrification north of Sevenoaks in 1935 resulted in an hourly local connecting service on the main line and a similar frequency on the branch. This was largely maintained until 19th September 1955 when off-peak services were withdrawn, Monday to Fridays. Thereafter Winter Sunday trains were also curtailed.

DUNTON GREEN and WESTERHAM

Second Class only, except where otherwise shown

May 1960

Miles from Dunton Green	Down — Week Days	a.m																											p.m
					SX		SO		SO	SX	SX	SO		SO	SO		SO		SO		SO		SO		SX		SO		SX
	65a Charing Cross . dep	..	6 27	..	7 20	..	7 21	..	7 57	7 53	8 37	8 37	..	1057	1157	..	1228	..	1 0	..	1 57	..	2 57	..	3 28	..	3 57	..	3 57
	65a Waterloo...... "	..	6 29	..	7 22	..	7 23	..	7 59	7 55	8 39	8 39	..	1059	1159	..	1230	..	1 2	..	1 59	..	2 59	..	3 30	..	3 59	..	3 59
	65a Cannon Street. "	5 8	6 27	..	7 15	..	7 37	..	7 41	7 38	8 25	8 45	..	1041	1141	..	1218	..	..	..	..	..	..	..	..	..	..	..	..
	65a London Bridge. "	5F45	6 35	..	7 26	..	7 41	..	8 4	7 59	8 43	8 48	..	11 4	12 4	..	1234	..	1 7	..	2 4	..	3 4	..	3 34	..	4 4	..	4 3
	Dunton Green...... dep	6 34	7 23	..	8 26	..	8 26	..	9 6	9 6	9 37	9 37	..	1150	1250	..	1 20	..	1 50	..	2 50	..	3 50	..	4 20	..	4 50	..	4 56
1¼	Chevening Halt.........	6 36	7 25	..	8 28	..	8 28	..	9 8	9 8	9 39	9 39	..	1152	1252	..	1 22	..	1 52	..	2 52	..	3 52	..	4 22	..	4 52	..	4 58
3¼	Brasted Halt..........	6 41	7 30	..	8 33	..	8 33	..	9 13	9 13	9 44	9 44	..	1157	1257	..	1 27	..	1 57	..	2 57	..	3 57	..	4 27	..	4 57	..	5 3
4¾	Westerham........ arr	6 45	7 34	..	8 37	..	8 37	..	9 17	9 17	9 48	9 48	..	12 1	1 1	..	1 31	..	2 1	..	3 1	..	4 1	..	4 31	..	5 1	..	5 7

Down	p.m — Week Days—continued																	p.m	a.m — Sundays					p.m
	SX		SO		SX		SX		SO		SX		SO		SX				F	F	F		F	F
65a Charing Cross . dep	4 27	..	4 57	..	5 11	..	5 30	..	5 57	..	6F28	..	6 57	..	6 57	..	..	..	6 57	7 57	8 57	EVERY HOUR (F) until 6 57 p.m. then at	7 57	8 57
65a Waterloo...... "	4 30	..	4 59	..	5 14	..	5 32	..	5 59	..	6F31	..	6 59	..	6 59	..	..	..	6 59	7 59	8 59		7 59	8 59
65a Cannon Street. "	4 28	..	..	..	5F30	..	..	..	..	..	6 4	..	..	..	6 57	..	..	..	..	..	..		..	..
65a London Bridge. "	4 34	..	5 4	..	5F33	..	5 36	..	6 4	..	6 7	..	7 4	..	7 4	..	..	..	7 4	8 4	9 4		8 4	9 4
Dunton Green...... dep	5 26	..	5 50	..	6 7	..	6 32	..	6 50	..	7 5	..	7 50	..	7 50	..	..	..	7 50	8 50	9 50		8 50	9 50
Chevening Halt.........	5 28	..	5 52	..	6 9	..	6 34	..	6 52	..	7 7	..	7 52	..	7 52	..	..	..	7 52	8 52	9 52		8 52	9 52
Brasted Halt	5 33	..	5 57	..	6 14	..	6 39	..	6 57	..	7 12	..	7 57	..	7 57	..	..	..	7 57	8 57	9 57		8 57	9 57
Westerham........ arr	5 37	..	6 1	..	6 18	..	6 43	..	7 1	..	7 16	..	8 1	..	8 1	..	..	..	8 1	9 1	10 1		9 1	10 1

Miles	Up — Week Days	a.m																											p.m
									SO	SX		SX	SO				SO			SO		SO		SO		SO			SO
	Westerham......... dep	6 10	..	6 59	..	7 38	..	8 10	8 40	8 44	..	9 21	9 21	9 52	..	..	1223	..	..	1 5	..	1 35	..	2 23	..	3 23	..	..	4 23
1½	Brasted Halt	6 13	..	7 2	..	7 41	..	8 13	8 43	8 47	..	9 24	9 24	9 55	..	..	1226	..	..	1 8	..	1 38	..	2 26	..	3 26	..	..	4 26
3½	Chevening Halt.........	6 18	..	7 7	..	7 46	..	8 18	8 48	8 52	..	9 29	9 29	10 0	..	..	1231	..	..	1 13	..	1 43	..	2 31	..	3 31	..	..	4 31
4¾	Dunton Green ...... arr	6 21	..	7 10	..	7 49	..	8 21	8 51	8 55	..	9 32	9 32	10 3	..	..	1234	..	..	1 16	..	1 46	..	2 34	..	3 34	..	..	4 34
23½	65a London Bridge. arr	7 8	..	7 53	..	8 33	..	8 52	9F23	9F23	..	10F 8	10 18	10 46	..	..	1 16	..	..	2 16	..	2 46	..	3 16	..	4 16	..	..	5 16
24	65a Cannon Street. "	7SX25	..	7 57	..	8 47	..	8 56	9F27	9F27	..	10F13	10F14	..	..	..		..	..	..	..		..	..	..	..	..	..	..
24½	65a Waterloo...... "	7 12	..	8 13	..	8 37	..	..	..	..	..	10 20	10 23	10 50	..	..	1 21	..	..	2 21	..	2 51	..	3 21	..	4 21	..	..	5 21
25¼	65a Charing Cross . "	7 14	..	8 17	..	8 42	..	..	..	..	..	10 22	10 26	10 53	..	..	1 24	..	..	2 24	..	2 53	..	3 24	..	4 24	..	..	5 24

Up	p.m — Week Days—continued																	p.m	a.m — Sundays						p.m
	SX		SX		SO		SX		SX		SO		SX		SO		SX		F	F	F		F		F
Westerham......... dep	4 42	..	5 12	..	5 23	..	5 49	..	6 21	..	6 23	..	6 47	..	7 23	..	7 23	..	8 23	9 23	1023	EVERY HOUR (F) until 7 23 p.m. then at	8 23	..	9 23
Brasted Halt	4 45	..	5 15	..	5 26	..	5 52	..	..	..	6 26	..	6 50	..	7 26	..	7 26	..	8 26	9 26	1026		8 26	..	9 26
Chevening Halt.........	4 50	..	5 20	..	5 31	..	5 57	..	..	..	6 31	..	6 55	..	7 31	..	7 31	..	8 31	9 31	1031		8 31	..	9 31
Dunton Green ...... arr	4 53	..	5 23	..	5 34	..	6 0	..	6 29	..	6 34	..	6 58	..	7 34	..	7 34	..	8 34	9 34	1034		8 34	..	9 34
65a London Bridge. arr	5 30	..	6 8	..	6 17	..	6 42	..	7 18	..	7 16	..	7 46	..	8 16	..	8 13	..	9 16	1016	1116		9 17	..	1019
65a Cannon Street. "	5 41	..	..	..	..	..	6 57	..	..	..	..	..	..	..	..	..	..	..	..	..	..		..	..	..
65a Waterloo...... "	5 35	..	6 13	..	6 22	..	6 47	..	7 22	..	7 21	..	7 51	..	8 21	..	8 22	..	9 21	1021	1121		9 22	..	1023
65a Charing Cross . "	5 38	..	6 17	..	6 24	..	6 49	..	7 25	..	7 24	..	7 55	..	8 24	..	8 25	..	9 25	1025	1124		9 25	..	1026

F Commences 20th March, 1960. F First and Second class. SO or S Saturdays only. SX or SX Saturdays excepted.

ORPINGTON

1. Until 1904, the station had only two platforms and was situated on the embankment south of the present station, seen here soon after completion. Rural Orpington then required cattle pens, evident in the right foreground. (Lens of Sutton)

2. Looking slightly to the left of the previous view, we see the large locomotive shed some time before electrification from London was initiated in 1925. This was built in about 1902 to house tank engines working suburban services. (Pamlin Prints)

3. Extension of quadruple track to Orpington in 1904 necessitated the construction of a new station with four through platforms and two bays at the London end, all of which are still in use today. This view of the country-end in the pre-electric era includes a fogman's hut. (Lens of Sutton)

4. These rather useless short sidings at the south end of the shed were removed soon after this photograph was taken on 14th February 1926. The building was still standing in 1992, partly in use as staff accommodation. The locomotives are nos. A521 and A662, 0-4-4Ts of class H and R respectively. (H.C.Casserley)

5. Electric services to Victoria commenced on 12th July 1925 and to Charing Cross and Cannon Street on 28th February 1926. Thereafter trains of this type provided the local service southwards. Ex-LSWR class M7 no.E131 stands by "A" Box shortly before electric traction was extended to Sevenoaks, services commencing on 6th January 1935. (Rev.A.W.V.Mace)

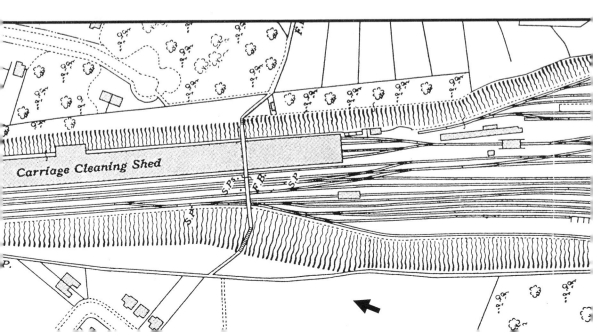

Carriage Cleaning Shed

6. Prior to the extension of electrification to Sevenoaks there was a length of electrified track southwards, which was used when electric trains were changing platforms. The conductor rail was longer than a train, in case the driver was slow in braking. "B" Box is seen at the south end of the platforms in 1948. (British Rail)

The 1933 survey shows the position of the redundant 55ft. turntable pit. The table had been moved to Horsham in 1927.

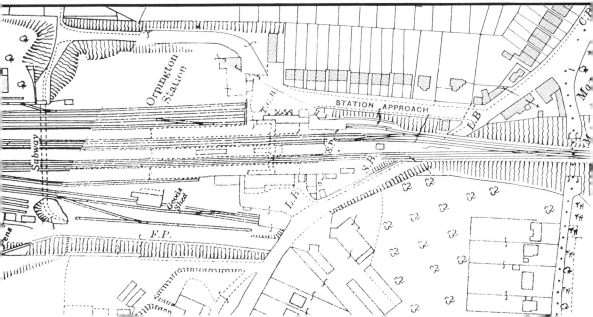

7. Standing under "A" Box in 1955 is one of the wooden framed 3-car electric sets into which a wider all-steel coach had been inserted. On the right is the goods yard, which closed on 7th October 1968. (British Rail)

8. For much of the 1950s, the 5.40pm from Cannon Street was first stop Knockholt and then all stations to Ashford. Hither Green Depot provided their solitary "King Arthur" class for this duty, no.30806 being seen here in excellent external condition. (N.Sprinks)

9. The northward view from "A" Box includes the unusual footbridge which passes through the roof of the "electric car shed". Berthing sidings were laid out here in about 1903 but the building was not erected until the advent of electrification. (British Rail)

10. Special narrow bodied diesel-electric six-car units were introduced on the Charing Cross-Hastings route in 1957. Their ponderous performance did nothing to help time-keeping on the line. No.1036 is bound for Hastings on 3rd April 1982, while no.1018 is destined for London. (J.Scrace)

11. Concrete segments for lining most of the Channel Tunnel were cast on the Isle of Grain (see *Branch Line to Allhallows*) and were usually hauled to Shakespeare Cliff by two class 33s. Nos.33020 and 33029 were performing this task on 18th July 1990. (J.S.Petley)

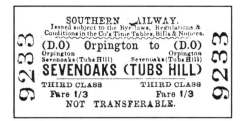

12. On the right is the signal box which replaced its two mechanical predecessors on 4th March 1962. In the centre is the carriage washer. Class 411 4CEP no.1602 forms part of an up train from Hastings, the route having been electrified in 1988. No.6205 is class 416/2 2EPB which will form part of a peak hour stopping service. (D.Brown)

CHELSFIELD

13. The station opened with the line due to cooperation with the local landowner, Mr. Waring. Its position was extremely unpopular and as a result of intensive agitation, an additional station was opened one mile southwards, nearer Halstead. Staggered platforms were typical of SER stations and are seen in about 1880. (Lens of Sutton)

The 1896 survey shows the sidings almost at their optimum, none being shown on the previous edition published in the 1860s. The village had a population of about 1500 at this time, its centre being one mile to the east.

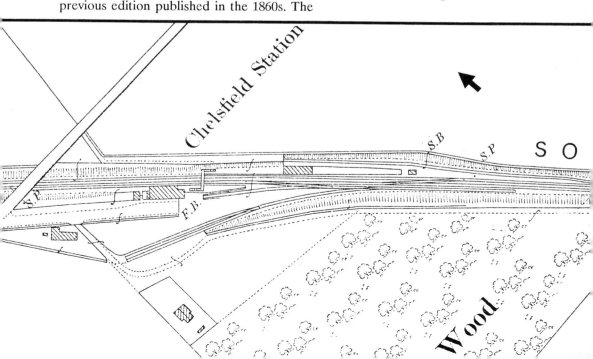

14. Another southward view, this time in 1934, emphasises the 1 in 118 gradient of the main line when compared with the level refuge siding on the left. (H.C.Casserley)

15. A down train arrives on 6th January 1934, headed by no.1595, one of a small batch of five J class 0-6-4Ts built in 1913 for the Hastings stopping trains. They were soon superseded by L class 4-4-0s. See picture 60 for a front view. (H.C.Casserley)

S. E. & C. R. (See Back
Available Day of issue ONLY.
CHELSFIELD to
ORPINGTON
2d   Second Class   2d
Orpington   Orpington
1658   1658

16. After 1935, this was a typical local train, its predecessor being illustrated on the cover of this album. North of Orpington, these 3SUB sets commonly worked in pairs with two former steam hauled coaches sandwiched between them. (D.Cullum coll.)

17. As a result of enemy action on 4th November 1940, the footbridge collapsed onto the leading coach of a 3SUB entering the down platform at 7.20pm. Both had been removed by the time that this photograph was taken on the following day. The bridge was rebuilt to the same design in 1941. (Lens of Sutton)

18. A 1954 southward view includes a footbridge passing only over coal sidings, an unusual arrangement. It was used by passengers destined for some places with equally unusual names - Pratt's Bottom, Worlds End and Julian's Brimstone, the latter being situated above the 597yd long Chelsfield Tunnel. The bridge was in use from about 1926 until 1970. (D.Cullum)

19. A 1954 northward view shows the limited extent of the headshunt to the goods yard, which closed on 18th April 1964. The signal box by the refuge sidings was in use until 13th May 1971 when it was destroyed by fire. At this time, one train started here on Mondays to Fridays, the 08.12 to Cannon Street. (D.Cullum)

20. The station buildings were also burnt down (in August 1973), apparently due to an electrical fault. A booking office within a glass box was considered to be the ideal replacement and is seen in 1990. (J.Scrace)

0652
12 | 11 | 10 | 9 | 8 | 7
SOUTHERN RAILWAY.
Issued subject to the Byelaws, Regulations &
Conditions in the Company's Bills and Notices.
CHELSFIELD
0652
The holder is prohibited from entering
the Company's Trains. Not Transferable.
Admit ONE to PLATFORM 1ᴰ
Available ONE HOUR on DAY of ISSUE ONLY
This ticket must be given up on leaving Platform
1 | 2 | 3 | 4 | 5 | 6

KNOCKHOLT

21. The station opened as Halstead on 1st May 1876, the village of about 600 souls being over one mile to the south. To avoid confusion with Halstead in Essex, the name was changed on 1st October 1900 to Knockholt, a village of about 900 people situated three miles to the south. (Lens of Sutton)

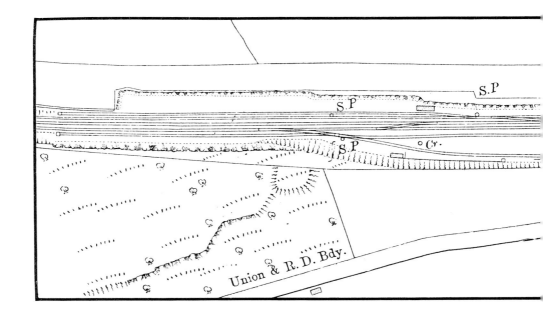

22. In most publications the name shown was "Halstead for Knockholt". Climbing at 1 in 170, a Stirling A class 4-4-0 with a down SER express approaches the summit of the three mile long climb from Orpington before plunging into the 1mile 851yd long Polhill Tunnel. (Lens of Sutton)

The 1909 map indicates the position of the crane (Cr.), which was of 5-ton capacity.

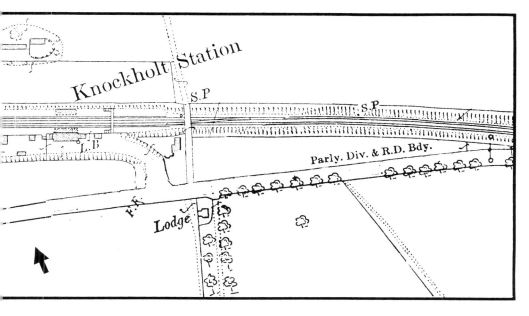

23. The sign proclaims "for Badgers Mount", another ambiguous name which would "fox" travellers from mainland Europe making their first journey in England. This is now an extensive residential area, one mile south-east of the station. This 1934 view includes the then common uninsulated telegraph wires. (H.C.Casserley)

24. A row of double telegraph poles flanks the deserted A21 on the left, the railway's system no longer carrying public traffic. The station approach road is also evident. The first signal box here was named "Wheatsheaf", opening with the line. The lattice footbridge was replaced in about 1970. (D.Cullum coll.)

25. The SER purchased additional land for a chalk quarry in 1898. This is the scene on 23rd March 1953 when it was reopened to supply material for sea defence work following the catastrophic floods in North Kent. Please see our *Sittingbourne to Ramsgate* album for illustrations of this massive undertaking. (British Rail)

26. A timber-framed building with weather board cladding was one of the standard economical forms of construction widely used by the SER. Many examples survived when this photograph was taken in 1954 but few now remain. (D.Cullum)

27. "Schools" class no.30936 *Cranleigh* roars up the incline past the quarry with a train for Dover, the up platform extension for the 1957 10-car suburban scheme being evident. Also included are the loading gauge and crane in the goods yard, which closed on 16th May 1964. (N.Sprinks)

28. Class H no.31552 and class C no.31715 were captured on their final journey, which was to Ashford on 4th November 1961 prior to scrapping. A drum of cable in a wagon to their rear symbolises the reason for their demise. The signal box closed on 1st August 1973. (S.C.Nash)

29. A fleet of fourteen electric locomotives was built for freight and boat train work in Kent, following the demise of steam. No.E5004 is coupled to a nuclear flask wagon on 11th September 1968. The pantograph was used under the wires erected at principal sidings. (J.Scrace)

SOUTHERN RAILWAY.
This ticket is not transferable and is issued subject to the Company's Bye-laws, Regulations and Conditions in their Time Tables, Notices and Book of Regulations.
Knockholt to
Knockholt
Charing Cross
Knockholt
Charing Cross
CHARING CROSS
FIRST CLASS
Fare 3/7
A/S
FIRST CLASS
Fare 3/7

30. The subsequent class 73 electro-diesels were more flexible, having a diesel option when leaving the third rail. No.73107 speeds through with the "Venice Simplon Orient Express", in which passengers would travel only as far as Folkestone, on 28th May 1985. In the background is the then new bridge for the link between the M25 and the A21 at Pratt's Bottom. (J.S.Petley)

31. The formation of Network SouthEast in 1986 resulted in the smartening of all stations and the rebuilding of some. Here is an example of the cottage style, an improvement on the earlier box-like structures. (J.Scrace)

32. "King Arthur" class no.801 *Sir Meliot de Logres* flies out of Polhill Tunnel on a down gradient of 1 in 143, leaving the Chalk of the North Downs behind it. This is just before electrification, as the insulators are shiny but the conductor rail is not. (R.S.Carpenter coll.)

33. The photographer turned and walked a few yards to record the up "Golden Arrow" behind no.863 *Lord Rodney*. Polhill Intermediate Box, which was closed on 4th March 1963, was situated on the other side of this road bridge. (R.S.Carpenter coll.)

DUNTON GREEN

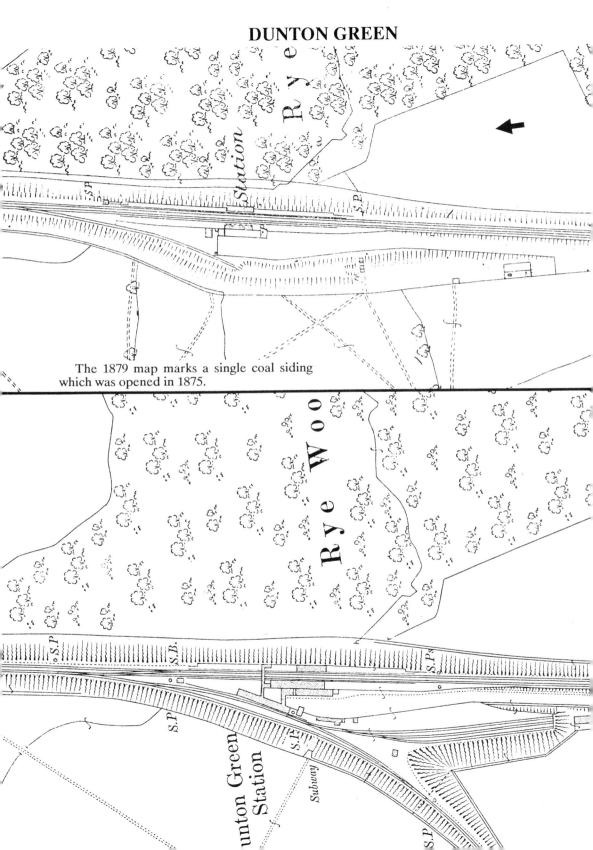

The 1879 map marks a single coal siding which was opened in 1875.

34. The station opened with the line and became a junction on 7th July 1881. The cantilevered signal box and the slotted signal post are seen ten years later. The footbridge was replaced by one previously in use at Grove Park. (Lens of Sutton)

The 1909 survey shows the junction arrangements which were little changed during the life of the Westerham branch. In earlier years the brickworks had more extensive sidings, which were worked by an Aveling and Porter geared locomotive. The works closed in 1965, having been operated by Wrefords since about 1920.

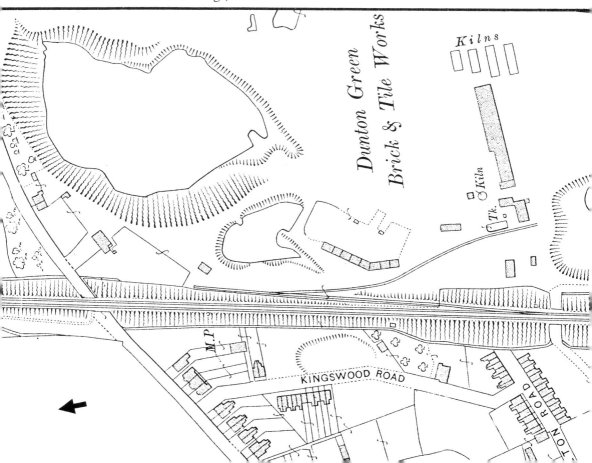

Dunton Green Brick & Tile Works

Kilns

Kiln

Tk.

M.P.

KINGSWOOD ROAD

TON ROAD

35. The SER was not noted for its consideration to passengers but here the footbridge was not only roofed but glazed. Study of the previous picture reveals that the latter was an afterthought and that the signal box position has been changed. This is a 1922 photograph. (H.J.Patterson Rutherford)

36. Subsequent to the transposition of the signal box, this curious and unique aerial ropeway was installed across the main lines for the conveyance of the single line tablet for the branch. Class B no.A458 is on the down line on 12th November 1927. (H.C.Casserley)

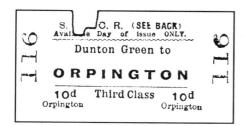

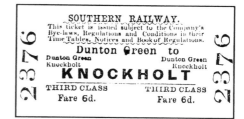

S.   C. R. (SEE BACK)
Available Day of Issue ONLY.

Dunton Green to

ORPINGTON

1 0d   Third Class   1 0d
Orpington   Orpington

116   116

SOUTHERN RAILWAY.
This ticket is issued subject to the Company's
Bye-laws, Regulations and Conditions in their
Time Tables, Notices and Book of Regulations.

Dunton Green to

Dunton Green   Dunton Green
Knockholt   Knockholt

KNOCKHOLT

THIRD CLASS   THIRD CLASS
Fare 6d.   Fare 6d.

2376   2376

37. The ramped walkway for tablet exchange is evident as class O1 no.1386 blows off in the branch platform on 11th March 1933. Subsequently tank engines were used almost exclusively on branch passenger services. (R.S.Carpenter coll.)

2nd · SINGLE   SINGLE · 2nd

Dunton Green to
Dunton Green   Dunton Green
Westerham   Westerham

WESTERHAM

(S)   1/-   FARE   1/-   (S)
For conditions see over   For conditions see over

1214   1214

SOUTHERN RAILWAY.
Issued subject to the Bye-laws, Regulations &
Conditions in the Company's Bills and Notices.

Dunton Green to
Dunton Green   Dunton Green
Chevening Halt   Chevening Halt

CHEVENING HALT

THIRD CLASS   THIRD CLASS
Fare 2½d.   Fare 2½d.
NOT TRANSFERABLE.

0098   0098

38. A June 1950 photograph includes a Bulleid Pacific by the up starting signal and the arched roof over the steps to the public subway, which passes under the tracks on the left. The subway dates from 1883. (D.Cullum)

39. Recorded in 1952 is this former steam railmotor body, dedicated to the branch for many years. Railmotors nos. 3 and 7 worked to Westerham between April 1906 and March 1907 but had insufficient capacity and were too slow when hauling an additional coach. (J.H.Aston)

40. This is the running-in board on the up platform in 1953, together with the assortment of huts that gradually grew around many stations in a less regulated age. (N.Sprinks)

41. A picture from May 1954 shows the plain concrete panel fencing provided by the SR and that gas lights were still in use. The tablet ropeway was abolished on 16th September 1934 and was replaced by a machine on the up platform. The platform extension on the right had been built in 1935. (D.Cullum)

SOUTHERN RAILWAY.

Dunton Green to

Dunton Green Sevenoaks (Tubs Hill)	Dunton Green Sevenoaks (Tubs Hill)
SEVENOAKS (TUBS HILL)	
THIRD CLASS	THIRD CLASS
Fare 3½d.	Fare 3½d.

FOR CONDITIONS SEE BACK.

3061

3061

42. Having just reversed, H class no.31520 is running onto the branch with the 11.17am empties from Tonbridge on 14th May 1960. The signal box remained in use until 2nd August 1973. (J.H.Aston)

43. Three more photographs from that fine May Saturday follow. There were no trains on the branch between 10.3am and 4.20pm on Mondays to Fridays at this time. No.31520 propels the 12.23 from Westerham and is arriving at 12.34 with motor set no.723. (J.H.Aston)

44. No.31520 is ready to return to Westerham at 12.50pm, while no.31500 waits to take over the branch service at 1.20, working through until 8.1pm. It is about to run onto the 16-chain curve which takes the line to a westerly direction. (J.H.Aston)

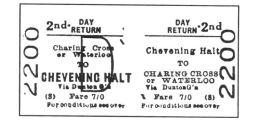

46. The last Westerham push-pull train departs for Tonbridge (empty) during the afternoon of 28th October 1961. The remaining trips were worked by a main line train owing to the size of the farewell crowds. (S.C.Nash)

45. With its old number of 500 highlighted in chalk, no.31500 departs for Westerham at 2.50pm. The roof over the subway steps (right) was still in place in 1992. (J.H.Aston)

47. Recorded in August 1970, the up building had been renovated and most of the huts had gone. The goods yard had closed on 2nd April 1962. (J.Scrace)

48. A special to Dover Western Docks speeds through on 27th September 1990, flanked by two modern waiting shelters. Although the chimneys have gone and windows have been boarded up, booking facilities were still available in the mornings. (J.Scrace)

BRANCH LINE TO WESTERHAM

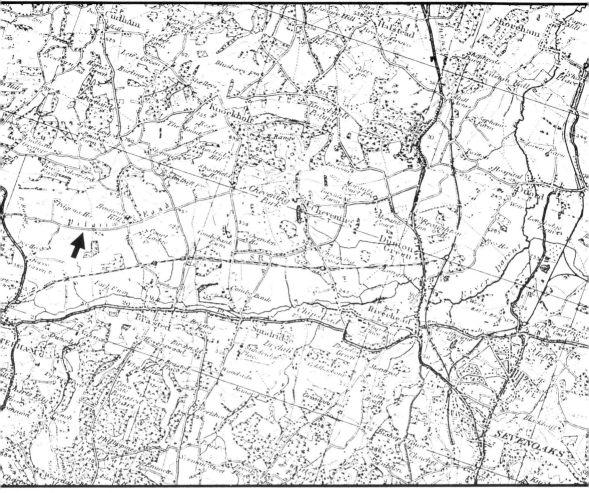

The 1930 map at 1" to 1 mile has the branch to Westerham from right to left. At the top is Halstead and nearby is Polhill Tunnel and the "Polhill Arms". On the right are the former LCDR lines and on the lower margin is Sevenoaks Tunnel. Between Dunton Green and Sevenoaks is Riverhead, which was the location of the 1927 accident, illustrated in picture no. 77. Lower left is "Chartwell", the home of Winston Churchill later to become Prime Minister.

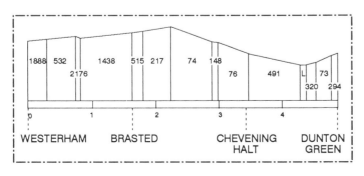

CHEVENING HALT

49. Seen near the halt on 3rd October 1936 was a rare example of a non-Eastern Section locomotive on the branch. Ex-LBSCR class D1 no. 2355 was a brief visitor. The lightweight SECR P class 0-6-0Ts had been used earlier on the branch, intermittently between 1909 and 1926. (H.C.Casserley)

50. The 2.55pm from Dunton Green on 11th April 1952 was formed of two former railmotor coaches, propelled by class R 0-4-4T no. 31675. The driving compartment also accommodated the guard, when there was one. (S.C.Nash)

51. For many years branch trains operated without guards, a junior porter from Dunton Green issuing bell-punch tickets to passengers joining the train here and at Brasted when unstaffed. The road bridge and the platform had been rebuilt after WWII, the latter having originally been of timber construction. (A.E.Bennett)

52. Although the open door is marked 1, first class had been abolished on the branch about 20 years before this photograph of H class no. 31500 was taken. The 2.50pm from Dunton Green is seen on 14th May 1960. (J.H.Aston)

BRASTED

53. Class O1 no. 1048 is standing near the station name which has been marked out with white stones. This class, along with B and B1 4-4-0s, came to the branch in 1926. Such tender engines were quite inappropiate to a route devoid of turntables. (D.Cullum coll.)

54. A 1957 view shows a busy goods yard. The rules of 1927 allowed the sidings to be shunted by a train from Westerham, returning there at 5.45am, propelling the wagons. In reality, the work would have probably been undertaken by a returning up train. (A.E.Bennett)

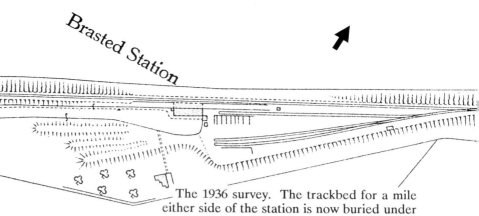

Brasted Station

The 1936 survey. The trackbed for a mile either side of the station is now buried under the M25. The solitary house was for the station master and was built in 1883 at a cost of £560.

55. All the points are in view as H class no. 31533 approaches the platform with set no. 732 on 1st October 1960. This class of locomotive was introduced to the branch for regular use in 1952. (T.Wright)

56. Two weeks before closure, coal was still being delivered to the yard. This closed with the line on 30th October 1961, although staffing ceased here in 1955. The population of the nearby village was about 1400 in the 1930s. (J.J.Smith)

WESTERHAM

57. The terminus was situated close to the town centre and adjacent to the main road to Bromley, left. This later became the A233. (Lens of Sutton)

58. In the distance is the engine shed built for the opening of the line to house a locomotive overnight. The necessity to do this ceased with the introduction of railmotors in 1906 and the shed was officially closed. However, it seems not to have been demolished until 1925. The locomotive is a Q class 0-4-4T, this class being in use on the branch from the 1890s to 1909. (B.Hart coll.)

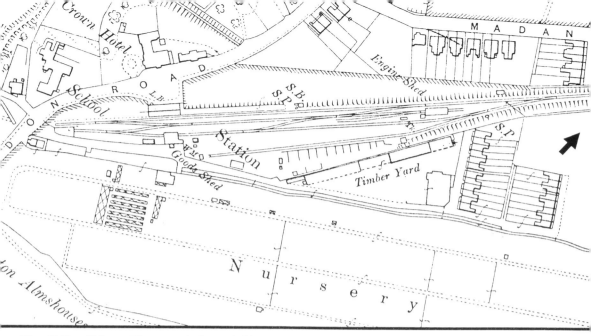

The 1909 edition. The population of this peaceful country town rose from only 2300 in 1881 to 3200 in 1921.

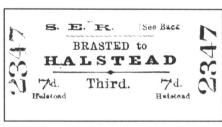

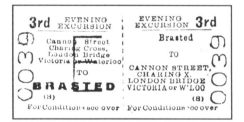

59. Class B no. A458 was one of the few not to be reboilered and become a B1. It is seen on 12th November 1927 coupled to ex-LCDR six-wheelers of dubious comfort. (H.C.Casserley)

60. Class J 0-6-4T no. A596 is seen on arrival with the second portion of a ramblers' excursion in about 1931. Another class J stands on the right, having worked the first portion in. (S.C.Nash coll.)

61. The 10.30am from Dunton Green on 14th March 1938 was hauled by ex-LCDR class R1 no. 1704. Kirtley's R and R1 locomotives were used regularly on the branch from 1933 until 1952. A Sentinel - Cammell steam railcar was tried in 1936. (J.R.W.Kirkby)

4364

SOUTHERN RAILWAY.
Available only for one journey
in either direction.
To be shown on demand.
THIRD CLASS SINGLE.
Fare 2½d
BETWEEN
Chevening Halt
AND
Dunton Green
This Ticket must be punched
opposite the Station or Halt
to which the Passenger is
entitled to travel.
FOR CONDITIONS
SEE BACK
Bell Punch Company, London. D5440

207
SOUTHERN RAILWAY.
CHEAP DAY
Available as advertised.
Bromley South to
BRASTED
Third Class
FOR CONDITIONS
SEE BACK
SOUTHERN RAILWAY.
CHEAP DAY
Available as advertised.
Brasted
Bromley
Brasted to
BROMLEY SOUTH
Third Class
173

S. E. R.
BRASTED to
BROMLEY Direct Route
1s.4½d. Third. 1s.4½d
Children over 3 and under 12 years
half fares under 3 years free.
Bromley   Bromley

62. Departing at 1.28pm on 11th April 1952 is R1 class no. 31704 seen in the previous picture, 14 years earlier. The intervening war had very little impact on the branch. (S.C.Nash)

63. From 1st January 1899 a joint managing committee operated the combined SER and LCDR. It was sometime before a new title was agreed and SE&CDR was used briefly, evidence of this remaining on a chair borne by a rotting sleeper in the yard in 1952. (J.H.Aston)

65. By 1957, the weather-boarded building was looking shabby, with some empty poster boards adding to the air of neglect. The bus and coach stops gleamed brightly, a direct service to Tonbridge being provided from the town centre. (A.E.Bennett)

64. On Tuesday 15th January 1957, no. 34017 *Ilfracombe* worked an eleven coach excursion to Kensington Olympia, probably for the Ideal Homes Exhibition. As the train was too long for the loop, another engine was provided at the far end, this being class D1 4-4-0 no.31487. (S.C.Nash)

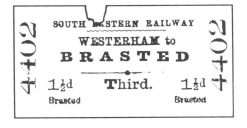

66. Included in this photograph from 10th September 1961 is the 5-ton capacity crane and the smartly painted Crown Hotel. Set 610 was one of 20 push-pull sets running at that time which had been created from ex-SR Maunsell corridor coaches. They replaced the ageing ex-railmotor sets. (J.Scrace)

67. The water tank and the 13-lever signal box continued to serve the line to the end, although the electric tablet system was abandoned in 1955 in favour of a "one engine in steam" train staff. Until that time, two trains were on the branch each evening - the 6.5 and 6.23 from Dunton Green.
(H.J.Patterson Rutherford)

68. Class H no.31520 takes water on Saturday 7th May 1960, between 1.1 and 1.5pm (in theory). The brick base of the wooden engine shed can still be seen, along with the outline of the inspection pit. The need for railings on the ruin is a mystery. (J.H.Aston)

3rd EARLY MORN-ING RETURN	EARLY MORN-ING RETURN **3rd**
0424 Surrey Docks TO **WESTERHAM** Via New Cross (S) Fare 3/2 For Conditions see over	Westerham TO **SURREY DOCKS** Via New Cross Fare 3/2 (S) For Conditions see over 0424

69. Although the counterweight bracket on the shunt signal featured in the previous picture was endorsed SE&CR, the tapered wooden post was probably of SER origin. It was one of the few still to be in use in 1961. (J.H.Aston)

70. The dock (right) could be used for end or side loading wagons, but for side access it was necessary for the vehicle to stand on the main line, an unusual arrangement. This is the end of the line, two weeks before the end of operations. (J.J.Smith)

WESTERHAM, BRASTED, and DUNTON GREEN.—Southern.

Miles.	Up.	mrn	mrn	mrn	mrn	mrn	mrn	mrn		aft	aft	aft	aft	aft	aft	aft	aft	aft	aft	aft	aft	aft
											S		E	S			S	E			W	M
	Westerham ....dep.	6 10	7 7	7 40	8 40	9 38	1040	1154	....	1 0	1 40	1552	4 0	2 55	3 55	4 45	5 22	6 16	6 50	7 45	9 20	1035	12 5
1½	Brasted	6 14	7 11	7 44	8 45	9 42	1044	1158	....	1 4	1 44	1592	4 4	2 59	3 59	4 49	5 26	6 29	6 54	7 49	9 24	1039	12 9
3½	Chevening Halt.....[256	6 18	7 15	7 ×4 8	50	9 46	1048	12 2	....	1 8	1 48	2 32	4 8	3 3	4 3	4 53	5 30	6 24	6 58	7 53	9 28	1043	1213
4½	Dunton Green 250, arr.	6 21	7 18	7 51	8 53	9 49	1051	12 5	....	1 10	1 51	2 62	5 13	6 4	6 4	5 65	5 33	6 27	7 1	7 56	9 31	1046	1216

WESTERHAM, BRASTED, and DUNTON GREEN.—Southern.

Up.	mrn	mrn	mrn	aft		aft	aft	aft	aft		aft	aft	aft		
Sundays.															
Westerham ....dep.	7 55	8 48	1050	12 4	....	12 47	3 55	5 25	6 45	....	9 0	8 24	9 20	....	**E** Except Saturdays.
Brasted	7 58	8 52	1054	12 8	....	12 50	3 59	5 28	6 49	....	9 4	8 38	9 24	....	**M** Mondays and Thursdays.
Chevening Halt................	8 3	8 56	1058	1212	....	12 55	4 3	5 33	6 53	....	9 8	8 42	9 28	....	**S** Saturdays only.
Dunton Green 253, 256..arr.	8 6	8 58	11 1	1215	....	12 58	4 6	5 36	6 56	....	9 11	8 45	9 31	....	**W** Wednesdays only.

July 1924

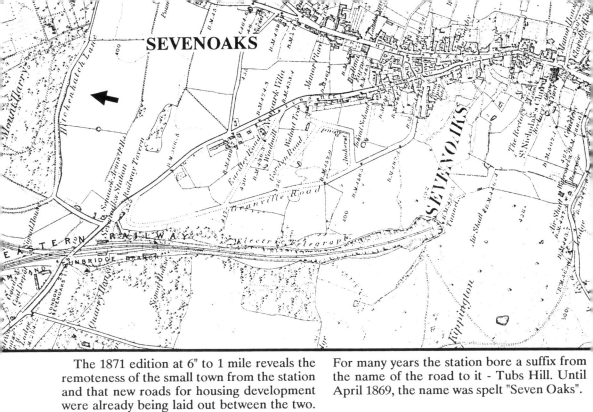

SEVENOAKS

The 1871 edition at 6" to 1 mile reveals the remoteness of the small town from the station and that new roads for housing development were already being laid out between the two.

For many years the station bore a suffix from the name of the road to it - Tubs Hill. Until April 1869, the name was spelt "Seven Oaks".

The 1937 survey has the line from Dunton Green lower left and the former LCDR route from Otford above it. The station had four

through lines from the outset. The railway helped the population grow from 6000 in 1871 to 11000 in 1931.

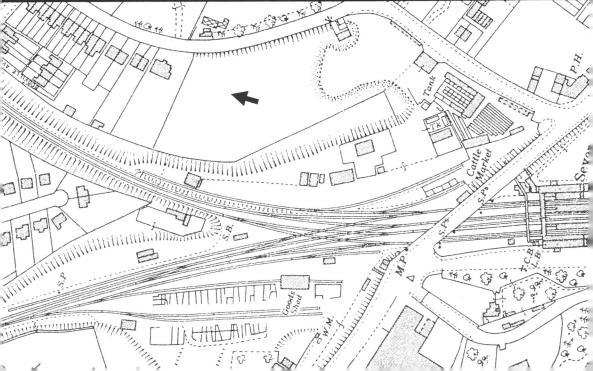

71. The first photograph of the station dates from 7th June 1884 when the 6.0pm goods from Deal ran into the rear of the 10.0pm goods from Folkestone, which was on the up fast line, slowly approaching the water column. A single block instrument was used for both up and down traffic, causing confusion between the signalman at Hildenborough, who was accused of negligence, and his colleague at Sevenoaks, who was considered to have lacked prompt action. (Lens of Sutton)

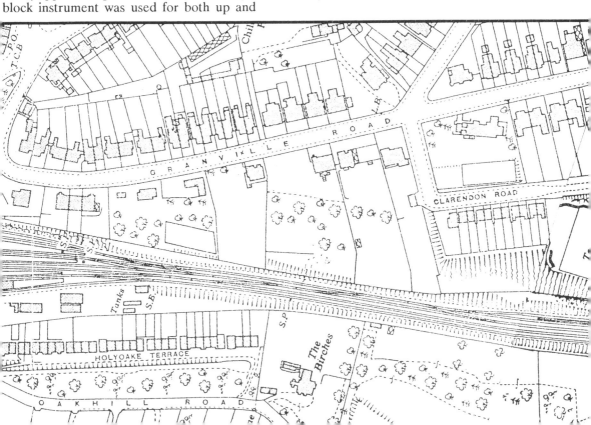

72. The crew of the leading engine from Deal died when 38 vans behind them piled up at 1.25am. The locomotives were 0-6-0s nos. 1 and 264. The Folkestone engine (0-6-0 no.294) was propelled 584yds following the impact. (H.C.Casserley coll.)

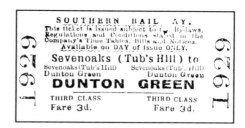

SOUTHERN RAILWAY.
This ticket is issued subject to the By-laws, Regulations and Conditions stated in the Company's Time Tables, Bills and Notices. Available on DAY of Issue ONLY.

Sevenoaks (Tub's Hill) to
Sevenoaks (Tub's Hill)   Sevenoaks (Tub's Hill)
Dunton Green   Dunton Green
DUNTON GREEN
THIRD CLASS   THIRD CLASS
Fare 3d.   Fare 3d.

73. A northward view from May 1890 includes the up bay. The LCDR was liable to a fee of £1000 per annum for the use of the station, but owing to non-payment their passenger trains were banned from 1st July 1886, although one goods transfer took place daily. Services were not resumed until the SECR was formed in 1899. They were suspended again during the later part of WWI as an economy measure. (Lens of Sutton)

74. Sevenoaks station was next in the news when, like many other towns, men were despatched with due ceremony to the battlefields of World War I. The train is in the down bay platform and could be bound for Shorncliffe. (Lens of Sutton)

75. Now named *Bluebell* and owned by the Bluebell Railway, P class 0-6-0T no.323 was working the "Otford Motor" when photographed on 3rd April 1926. (H.C.Casserley)

76. Recorded on the same day, class D no. A488 is leaving the station through the sandstone strata of the Hythe Beds with a down train. A carriage berthing siding is on the right, coaches being evident in the distance. In 1962 this was made into two separate sidings. The water from Sevenoaks Tunnel was utilised by the Sevenoaks Water Co. from its inception in 1871. (H.C.Casserley)

77. On 24th August 1927 "River" class 2-6-4T no. A800 was working the 5.0pm Cannon Street to Deal when it started to roll violently after passing over the points to Dunton Green brickworks. The locomotive derailed and several coaches hit the pier of Shoreham Lane bridge, 13 lives being lost. Contributory factors included poor track level (too low by 1.44"), bad track drainage, poor ballast and dubious features of locomotive design. Subsequently the entire class was rebuilt as 2-6-0s with tenders instead of high side tanks. (A.R.Lambert)

78. Owing to the limited space in the compartments, luggage vans were always incorporated into trains running in connection with cross-Channel ferries. *Lord Nelson* no. E850 is seen in 1928, prior to the fitting of the familiar smoke deflectors. The ground signal and the perforated concrete signal post are long lost features. (P. Ransome Wallis)

79. "Lord Nelson" class no. E852 *Sir Walter Raleigh* developed a hot axle box while working an up Continental Express one day in May 1929 and had to be taken off into the goods yard. Local schoolboy, Arthur Lloyd Lambert clearly relishes the opportunity of close proximity to a static Nelson. (D.G.Sheffield)

80. Class B1 4-4-0 ("Flying Bedstead") no. 1101 simmers on the down slow line on 6th January 1934. The advertisement proclaims "Summer PENNY A MILE RETURN TICKETS" while the nameboard shows the words "Tubs Hill", used to distinguish it from the ex-LCDR station - "Bat & Ball". (H.C.Casserley)

81. A post-WWII 4SUB waits near C class 0-6-0 no. 31510, which was in traffic until 1962. The 1937 map shows two footbridges. The second was of iron lattice construction and was demolished in 1947. (Lens of Sutton)

82. Now follow three photographs taken on 23rd May 1955, this one including the then new footbridge between platforms 5 and 6, together with two styles of gas light. The platform canopies had been erected during improvements in 1935. (D.Cullum)

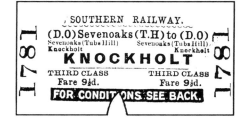

SOUTHERN RAILWAY.
(D.O)Sevenoaks(T.H) to (D.O)
Sevenoaks(Tubs Hill)   Sevenoaks(Tubs Hill)
Knockholt   Knockholt
KNOCKHOLT
THIRD CLASS   THIRD CLASS
Fare 9½d.   Fare 9½d.
FOR CONDITIONS SEE BACK.
1781   1781

83. A southwards view includes gas lights (nearing the end of their lives), two water tanks (for locomotive supply), two berthing sidings (for local electric trains), a conductor rail on the down line beyond the crossover (to allow terminating electrics to transfer to an up platform), "B" Box and the up refuge siding which was not electrified. (D.Cullum)

84. The North Downs are in the background and the former LCDR route to Otford is on the right, as no. 34083 *605 Squadron* approaches the multitude of diamond crossings with the 1.15pm Charing Cross to Dover express. The goods yard, which had a 7½ ton crane, closed on 2nd October 1972 having only handled coal since 4th September 1965. Most of the sidings were lifted in 1975. (D.Cullum)

85. The red banner on the left indicates that the down berthing sidings were temporarily out of use on 28th July 1956, as "Schools" class no. 30928 *Stowe* hurries towards London with a train from Dover. This locomotive is now to be found on the Bluebell Railway. (A.E.Bennett)

86. In 1957 the platforms were lengthened as far as "B" Box and electric lighting was provided. The full service of DEMUs on the Hastings route commenced in 1958, the unique fleet operating until 1988, when electrification took place. (English Electric)

87. Although electrification to Dover took place on 12th June 1961, some trains were subsequently steam hauled owing to a shortage of new stock. Thus the old timetable was still in operation in September 1961 as no. 7138 waits for departure time (12.51 to Charing Cross) and the 12.49 departure for Ashford is loco hauled (no. E5013), as there are vans behind the three coaches. (A.Ll.Lambert)

89. Renovation was in progress on 23rd February 1990 as no. 60006 was passing on a crew training trip, prior to the replacement of pairs of class 33s on Channel Tunnel construction trains. Part of the old platform 6 was retained (right) for mail traffic, but this had ceased by then. (J.S.Petley)

88. The choice of direct destinations increased on 16th May 1988, when an hourly Thameslink service to Cricklewood via Otford and Catford commenced. The 12.51 departure is seen on 6th December 1989. When the station was rebuilt in 1976 the old platforms 1 and 6 were closed and a number of small shops were incorporated into the new entrance, left. (C.Wilson)

90. Further platform improvements and lengthening were in hand as refurbished 4CEP no. 1595 leaves for Hastings on 20th February 1991. At platform 4 an elderly 4EPB waits to depart for Blackfriars via the ex-LCDR route. At this time, the up berthing siding was removed and the up loop lengthened in readiness for the Three-Capitals trains. (M.Turvey)

SOUTH OF SEVENOAKS

92. Half a mile from the station the line enters the longest tunnel on the former SR, Sevenoaks Tunnel, which is 1 mile 1693 yds (or nearly two miles) long. The tunnel is on a 1 in 144 down gradient to the south portal, half a mile beyond which was Weald Intermediate Box, seen here as empty stock passes from Tonbridge for the Westerham branch. (N.Sprinks)

←——

91. This signal box replaced the two mechanical ones on 4th March 1962. No. 73103 stands at platform 2 with an engineers train on 21st February 1992, up trains being able to start from any of the four platforms. (V. Mitchell)

93. Looking back towards the tunnel we see the topography that necessitated it and the gate to the goods yard which closed on 2nd October 1961. The signal box was abolished on 4th March 1962. (D.Cullum)

The 1936 survey marks the siding which was available for public traffic and also used by the tunnel engineers.

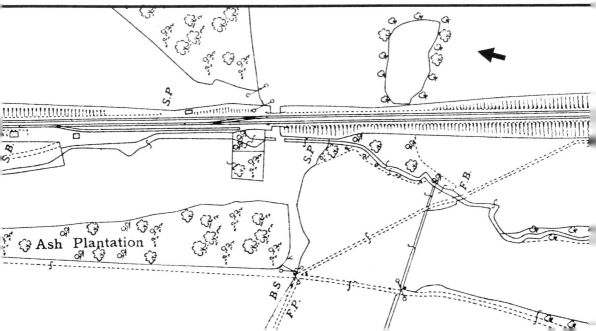

Ash Plantation

HILDENBOROUGH

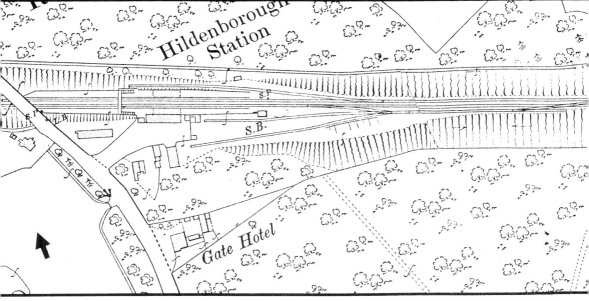

The 1908 map marks the down refuge siding,
barely visible in any of the photographs.

94. The passenger station opened with this section of the line on 1st May 1868 but goods facilities were deferred until about 1872, due to excessive demands by the landowner. This view from around 1875 includes an early double-armed signal. (Lens of Sutton)

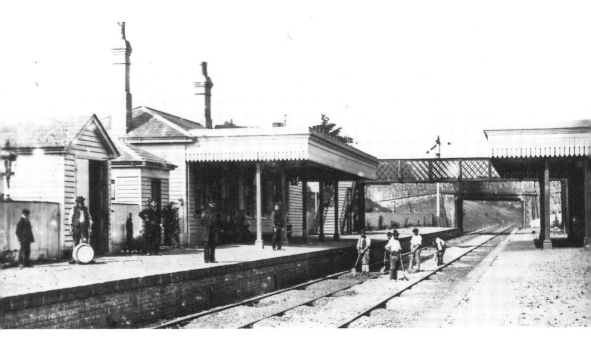

95. Southbound is class E no. A516, the "A" indicating that Ashford Works was its location for major overhauls, in common with other former SECR engines. Leading is a three-coach birdcage set, so called because of the raised lookouts for guards. (D.Cullum coll.)

96. This is a southward view down the 1 in 122 gradient to the Medway Valley in February 1952. The station was about one mile from the village, which had about 1400 inhabitants in 1900. (D.Cullum)

97. "Britannia" class no.70004 *William Shakespeare* was regularly used on the important Golden Arrow Pullman train, which ran until 30th September 1972, although electrically hauled from 1961. The second van in this photograph from 18th July 1953 carries baggage boxes of registered luggage and mails, which were conveyed in the hold of the ferry. (N.Sprinks)

98. Passing the short up goods run round on 4th November 1961 are two locomotives on their last workings before scrapping. They are class D1 no.31749 of 1903 and class E1 no.31067 from 1908. The train is a permanent way special. The goods yard had closed on 5th October 1960 and the signal box (left) followed on 4th March 1962. (S.C.Nash)

99. The south facade is seen in August 1990 by which time the old structure had been subjected to refurbishment, formerly known as modernisation. At least it had not been boarded up or demolished. (J.Scrace)

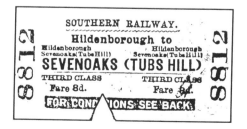

100. The platform canopy was still in place on 8th March 1991 as no.56060 runs downhill with aggregate for Channel Tunnel work. This was loaded at Grain, where it was received by sea from Glensanda Quarry, on the west coast of Scotland. (J.S.Petley)

101. A 22-chain curve north of the junction with the main line (Redhill-Ashford), necessitates speed restrictions (40mph for down trains, 50 for up) and deprives up trains of a run at the continuous rising gradient to Sevenoaks Tunnel. "Schools" class no.30919 *Harrow* rounds the curve with the 1.40pm Hastings to Charing Cross on 15th March 1953, before crossing the River Medway. (N.Sprinks)

102. Leaving Tonbridge on 24th June 1953 is no.35026 *Lamport and Holt Line* with through mail vans and sleeping cars from Paris Nord via the Dunkirk-Dover ferry. In later years this train conveyed sleepers from Brussels and also Basle. A buffet car and ordinary coaches were attached at the rear for those of more limited means. (N.Sprinks)

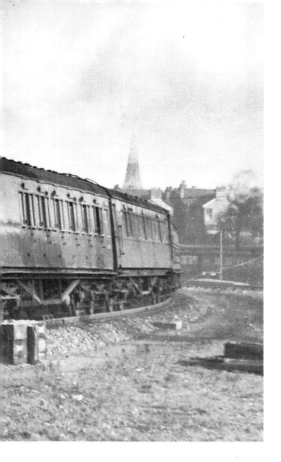

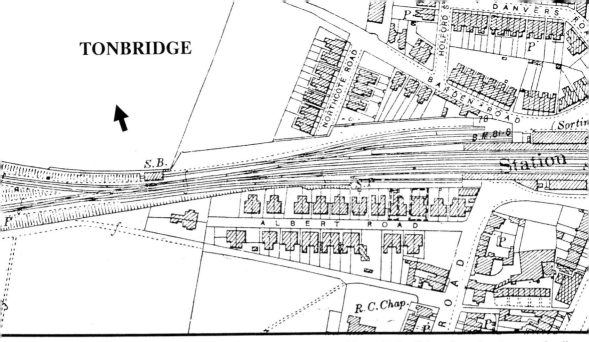

TONBRIDGE

The 1897 edition has the Sevenoaks line above that from Redhill on the left. On the right is the route to Ashford, with the Hastings line bottom right.

103. The station opened as "Tunbridge" in 1842 and became the junction for Tunbridge Wells in 1851, being renamed "Tunbridge Junction" in the following year. It became "Tonbridge Junction" in 1893 and assumed its present name in 1929. Passing East Box is an F class 4-4-0 with the down Dover Club Train, which ran from 1889 to 1892. (D.Cullum coll.)

104. A local train stands in the down bay as a stopping train arrives at the down through platform, which appears to have more staff than passengers. The two through lines for expresses were a feature of the station from its inception. (Lens of Sutton)

105. On 5th March 1909, the Dover Pier boat train ran in two parts from Charing Cross - 8.40am via Redhill and 9.0am via Cannon Street and Orpington, both hauled by E class 4-4-0s. At 9.57, the engine of the latter (no.497) struck the tender of the former (no.165) on the junction, resulting in the death of two railwaymen and immense embarrassment to the SECR, as His Majesty King Edward VII was travelling in a following train. This had to be reversed at Orpington and sent to Dover via Chatham. (Lens of Sutton)

106. An up express speeds through in the summer of 1913, "birdcage" lookouts being much in evidence. A source of danger for station staff was this crossing over four running lines, especially with a heavy case on one shoulder obstructing vision. Wainwright D class 4-4-0 no.247 was the only one fitted with an extended smokebox.
(H.J.Patterson Rutherford coll.)

107. Class O1 no.1432 takes a run at the climb out of Tonbridge with the 10.0am goods to Tunbridge Wells Central and West on 19th September 1938. Most goods trains were banked up this line, the exhaust of the banking engine being seen on the left. (J.R.W.Kirkby)

108. In 1935, the platforms were rebuilt, new canopies provided and the up bay altered and provided with a through line. "Schools" class no. 934 *St. Lawrence* runs past the new platforms, not long after they were completed. The tracks through the station were realigned to allow the speed restriction on the Sevenoaks line to be raised. (R.S.Carpenter coll.)

Other maps and photographs of this important junction are included in our *Redhill to Ashford* and *Tonbridge to Hastings* albums.

←

109. With the Redhill lines on the left, "Schools" class no. 30927 *Clifton* swings round the curve from Sevenoaks bound for Folkestone having passed West Box, by then designated "A" Box. A panel box was built nearby and opened on 18th March 1962, superseding both "A" and "B" Boxes. (C.R.L.Coles)

110. The 7.10pm Tunbridge Wells West to Charing Cross on 20th June 1953 was composed entirely of ex-SECR stock, L class no. 31764 having been built in 1914. The train is about to pass the extensive West Yard, laid out between the old and new main lines of the SER, during WWII. (N.Sprinks)

111. The 1.10pm Ostend boat train from Dover Marine to Victoria passes Tonbridge on the up through line on 11th October 1953, behind "Battle of Britain" 4-6-2 no.34074 *46 Squadron*. During the winter service at this time, this train normally combined at Folkestone Junction with a Calais-Folkestone boat train, but on this day heavy traffic off the Calais ship necessitated the trains running separately. The 2.44 Tonbridge to Redhill is signalled to depart from platform 1. (N.Sprinks)

112. While a local train stands in platform 4, the 14.29 Ramsgate - Dover Priory - Charing Cross brakes ready to take the curve to Sevenoaks on 18th April 1985, the year before NSE livery was introduced. The narrow arches of the road bridge have alarmingly limited clearances. (D.Brown)

113. For many years the Tonbridge - Reading services were operated by "Tadpole" sets of this type. However this one has a Hampshire driving trailer (left) coupled to two Hastings line vehicles, hence the 1066 logo. It is working empty to St. Leonards on 4th April 1986. (C.Wilson)

114. Direct freight from mainland Europe via the train ferries has run through Tonbridge since 1936, war years excepted. This is the Dover - Glasgow service on 3rd November 1988. Mail traffic is also evident, this recently having been boosted with the introduction of a Dover - Manchester travelling post office each night. (J.Scrace)

115. The unimposing entrance does not reflect the importance of the station for revenue. For example, over 6000 season tickets were issued back in 1932. Alterations in 1935 resulted in the loss of the round headed windows and the ornate stone balustrade along the roof line. Recent tiling disguises this historic building. (J.Scrace)

TONBRIDGE SHED

116. The map shows the position of the engine shed, east of the main road. Its predecessor was slightly further east. Outside the shed on 17th July 1926 are nos. 94 and 96 of class F1 and O respectively. (H.C.Casserley)

117. Taking water on 20th August 1927 is class B1 no. 451 built in 1898 as class B and rebuilt in 1915. On the left is East Box which controlled the junction of the Hastings and Ashford lines until 1935. (H.C.Casserley)

118. The road bridge is in the background of this and the previous picture, but here we see the framework for the new East Box under construction on 22nd October 1934. This ex-SER class R has Stirling's rounded cab, but not the short chimney fitted to other members of this small class for working through the restricted tunnel between Canterbury and Whitstable. (H.C.Casserley)

119. On the south side of the shed was the 55ft turntable, operated by vacuum from the engine - note the connecting hose from the class D1, seen turning on 11th May 1957. At its peak, in the 1930s, this shed was allocated over 50 engines. (F.Hornby)

120. New brick gables and an asbestos roof were provided in 1952 but, ten years later, there were fewer than ten engines left. This view of the east end on 16th August 1960 included Q1s no. 33001 (now preserved) and 33039, together with class N1 no. 31876. The end of steam here in June 1964 was fortunately preceded by a marked improvement in passenger services to London, which has since been largely maintained. (J.Scrace)

MP Middleton Press

Easebourne Lane, Midhurst. West Sussex. GU29 9AZ
Tel: (0730) 813169   Fax: (0730) 812601

Write or telephone for our latest booklist

BRANCH LINES

BRANCH LINES TO MIDHURST
BRANCH LINES AROUND MIDHURST
BRANCH LINES TO HORSHAM
BRANCH LINE TO SELSEY
BRANCH LINES TO EAST GRINSTEAD
BRANCH LINES TO ALTON
BRANCH LINE TO TENTERDEN
BRANCH LINES TO NEWPORT
BRANCH LINES TO TUNBRIDGE WELLS
BRANCH LINE TO SWANAGE
BRANCH LINE TO LYME REGIS
BRANCH LINE TO FAIRFORD
BRANCH LINE TO ALLHALLOWS
BRANCH LINES AROUND ASCOT
BRANCH LINES AROUND WEYMOUTH
BRANCH LINE TO HAWKHURST
BRANCH LINES AROUND EFFINGHAM JN
BRANCH LINE TO MINEHEAD
BRANCH LINE TO SHREWSBURY
BRANCH LINES AROUND HUNTINGDON
BRANCH LINES TO SEATON AND SIDMOUTH
BRANCH LINES AROUND WIMBORNE
BRANCH LINES TO EXMOUTH

SOUTH COAST RAILWAYS

CHICHESTER TO PORTSMOUTH
BRIGHTON TO EASTBOURNE
RYDE TO VENTNOR
EASTBOURNE TO HASTINGS
PORTSMOUTH TO SOUTHAMPTON
HASTINGS TO ASHFORD
SOUTHAMPTON TO BOURNEMOUTH
ASHFORD TO DOVER
BOURNEMOUTH TO WEYMOUTH
DOVER TO RAMSGATE

COUNTRY RAILWAY ROUTES

BOURNEMOUTH TO EVERCREECH JN
READING TO GUILDFORD
WOKING TO ALTON
BATH TO EVERCREECH JUNCTION
GUILDFORD TO REDHILL
EAST KENT LIGHT RAILWAY
FAREHAM TO SALISBURY
BURNHAM TO EVERCREECH JUNCTION
REDHILL TO ASHFORD
YEOVIL TO DORCHESTER
ANDOVER TO SOUTHAMPTON

SOUTHERN MAIN LINES

HAYWARDS HEATH TO SEAFORD
EPSOM TO HORSHAM
CRAWLEY TO LITTLEHAMPTON
THREE BRIDGES TO BRIGHTON
WATERLOO TO WOKING
VICTORIA TO EAST CROYDON
EAST CROYDON TO THREE BRIDGES
WOKING TO SOUTHAMPTON
WATERLOO TO WINDSOR
LONDON BRIDGE TO EAST CROYDON
BASINGSTOKE TO SALISBURY
SITTINGBOURNE TO RAMSGATE
YEOVIL TO EXETER
CHARING CROSS TO ORPINGTON
VICTORIA TO BROMLEY SOUTH
ORPINGTON TO TONBRIDGE

LONDON SUBURBAN RAILWAYS

CHARING CROSS TO DARTFORD
HOLBORN VIADUCT TO LEWISHAM
KINGSTON & HOUNSLOW LOOPS
CRYSTAL PALACE AND CATFORD LOOP
LEWISHAM TO DARTFORD
MITCHAM JUNCTION LINES

STEAMING THROUGH

STEAMING THROUGH EAST HANTS
STEAMING THROUGH SURREY
STEAMING THROUGH WEST SUSSEX
STEAMING THROUGH THE ISLE OF WIGHT
STEAMING THROUGH WEST HANTS

OTHER RAILWAY BOOKS

GARRAWAY FATHER & SON
LONDON CHATHAM & DOVER RAILWAY
INDUSTRIAL RAILWAYS OF THE S. EAST
WEST SUSSEX RAILWAYS IN THE 1980s
SOUTH EASTERN RAILWAY

OTHER BOOKS

WALKS IN THE WESTERN HIGH WEALD
TILLINGBOURNE BUS STORY
MILITARY DEFENCE OF WEST SUSSEX
BATTLE OVER SUSSEX 1940
SURREY WATERWAYS
KENT AND EAST SUSSEX WATERWAYS
HAMPSHIRE WATERWAYS